HANG-UPS

Roy Mitchell

Ward Lock Limited · London

DEDICATED TO MY FATHER

First published in Great Britain in 1985
by Ward Lock Limited, 82 Gower Street,
London WC1E 6EQ, an Egmont Company.

Typeset by Ampersand Communication, London

Printed and bound in Great Britain by Hollen Street Press, Slough

British Library Cataloguing in Publication Data

Mitchell, Roy
    Hang-ups
    1. English wit and humour, Pictorial
    I. Title
    741.5'942   NC1479

ISBN 0-7063-6423-6

'Are you hanging comfortably?'

'OK, so we've got a cake with a file in it – now what?'

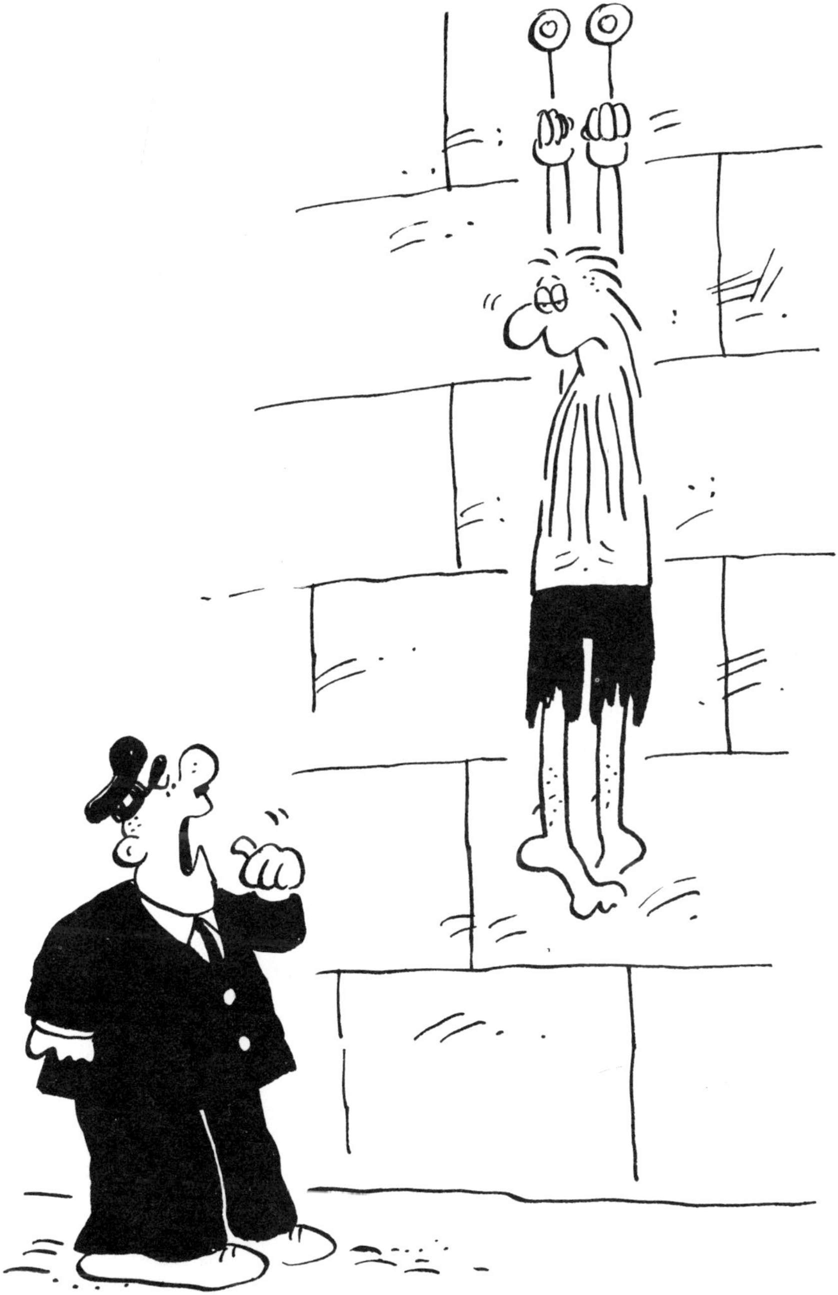

'Is that *your* car blocking me in?'

'...And just keep your hands to yourself!'

'Don't forget to thank the governor for the wellies...'

'...A film...Three words...First word "The"...'

'Funny, isn't it, how Monday always drags...'

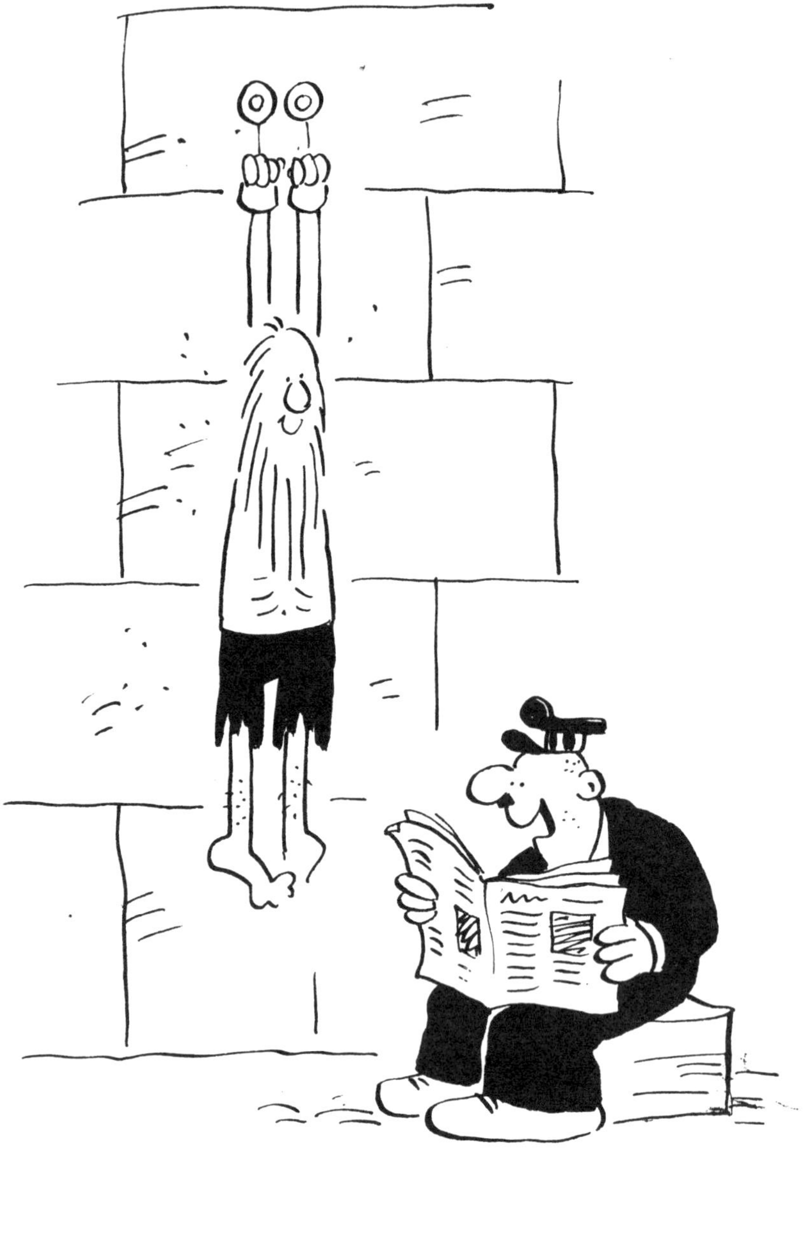

'Taurus? – "You will be lucky in love, and the time is right for making new plans" ...'

'Perhaps the time would pass more quickly if you had a little hobby...'

'So you let him pull the wishbone – *then* what?'

'That beard definitely makes you look older...'

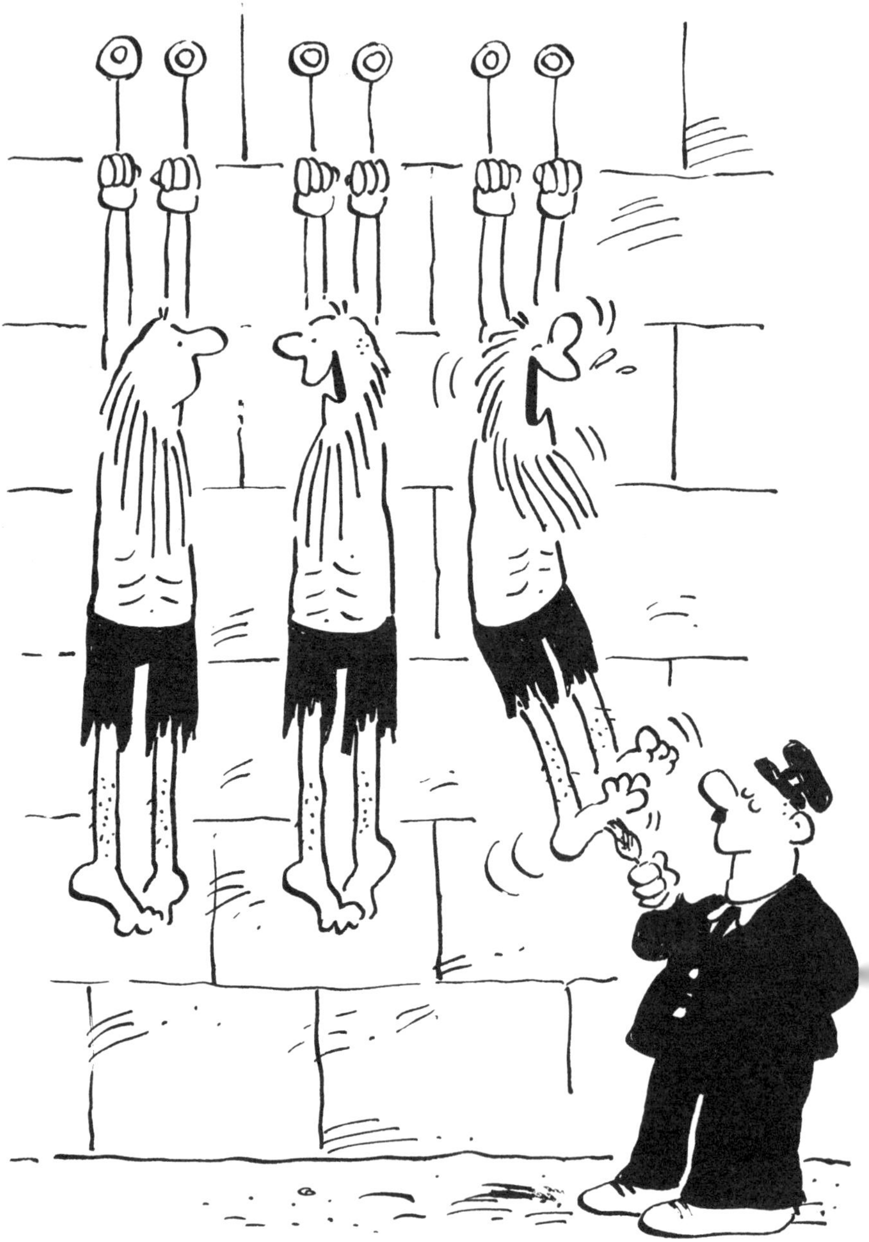

'It's his birthday.'

'Boy, do I feel lucky today!'

'Not very generous, are they?'

'Can we have our ball back, Mister?'

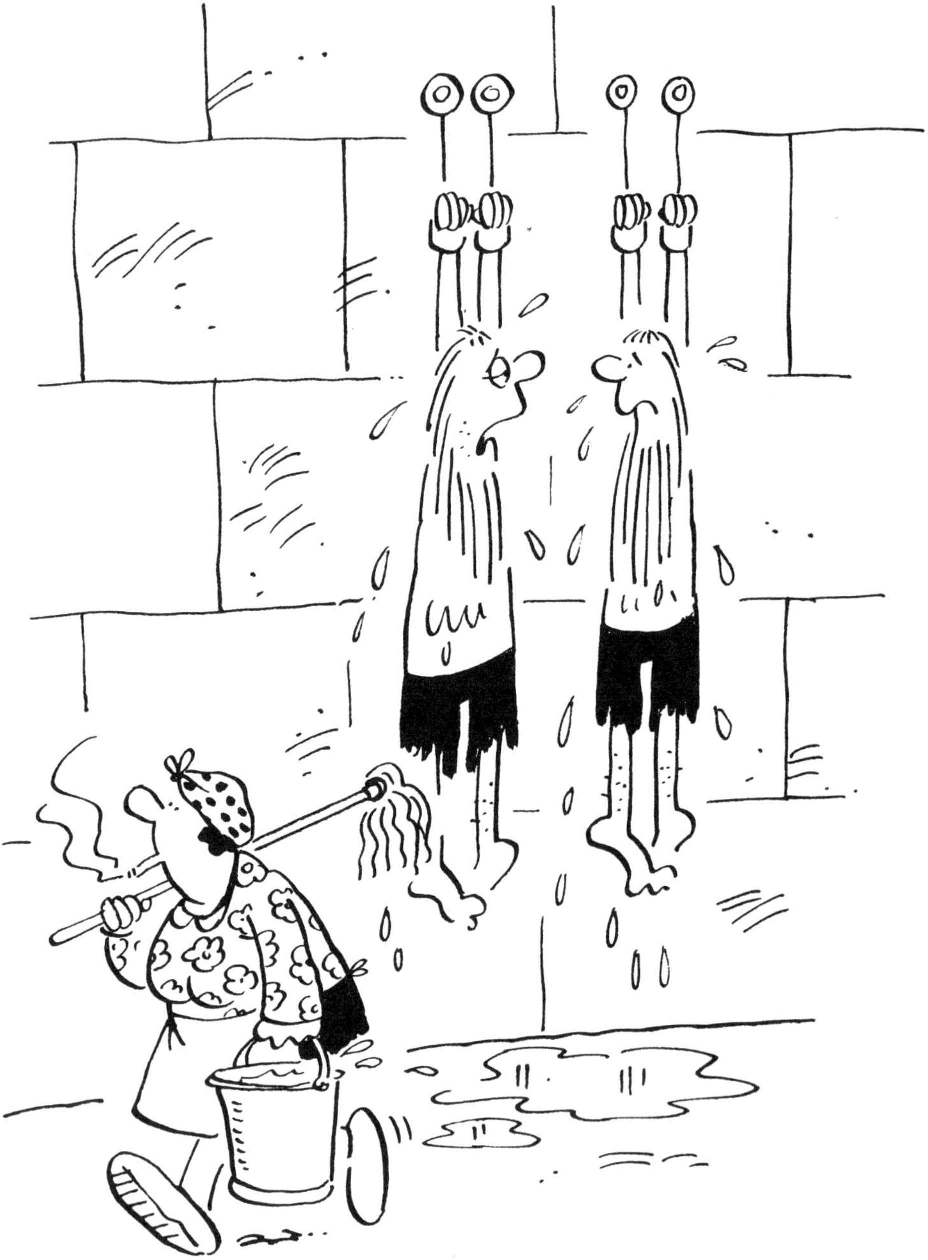

'I hate bath night...'

'You and your stupid bird impressions!'

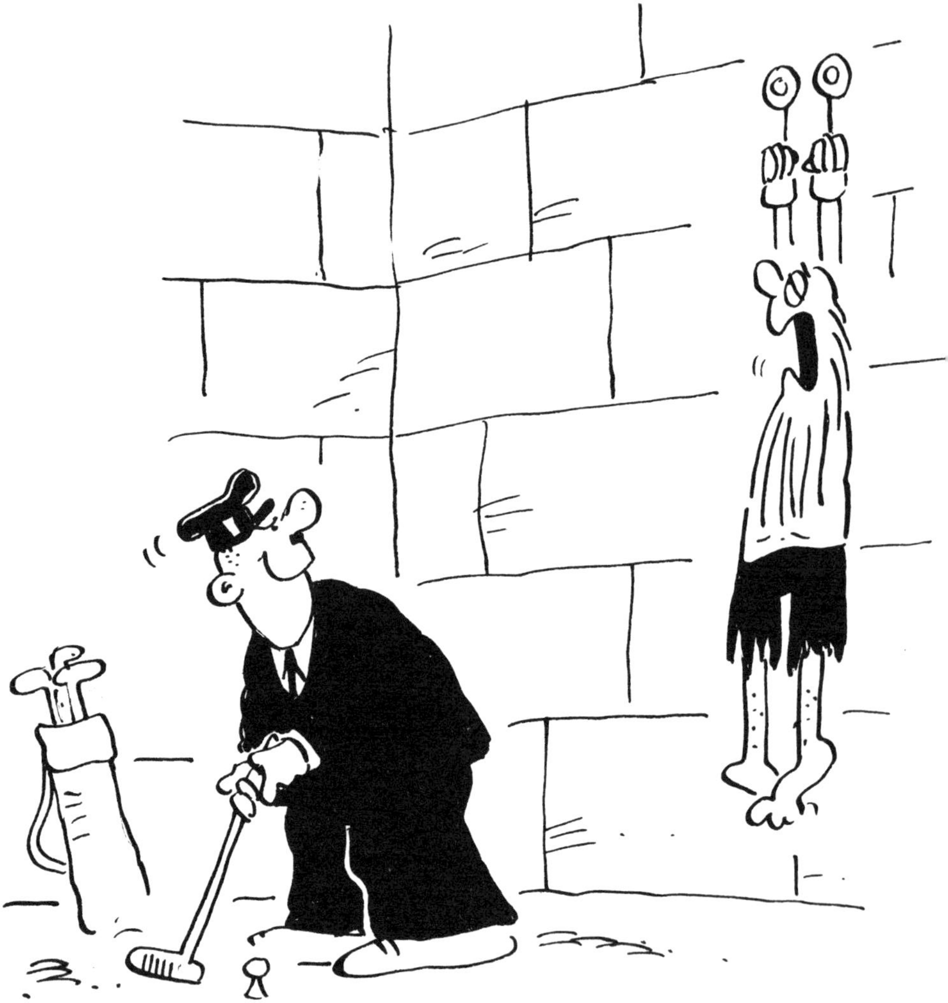

'It sort of grows on you after a while...'

'You've got to admire his optimism, haven't you?'

'Don't look now, but your flies are undone...'

'I *told* you not to ask him to scratch your nose!'

'Dammit! – I've lost a contact lens!'

'One day we'll look back and have a real good laugh about this...'

'Same here – I've not had a minute all day...'

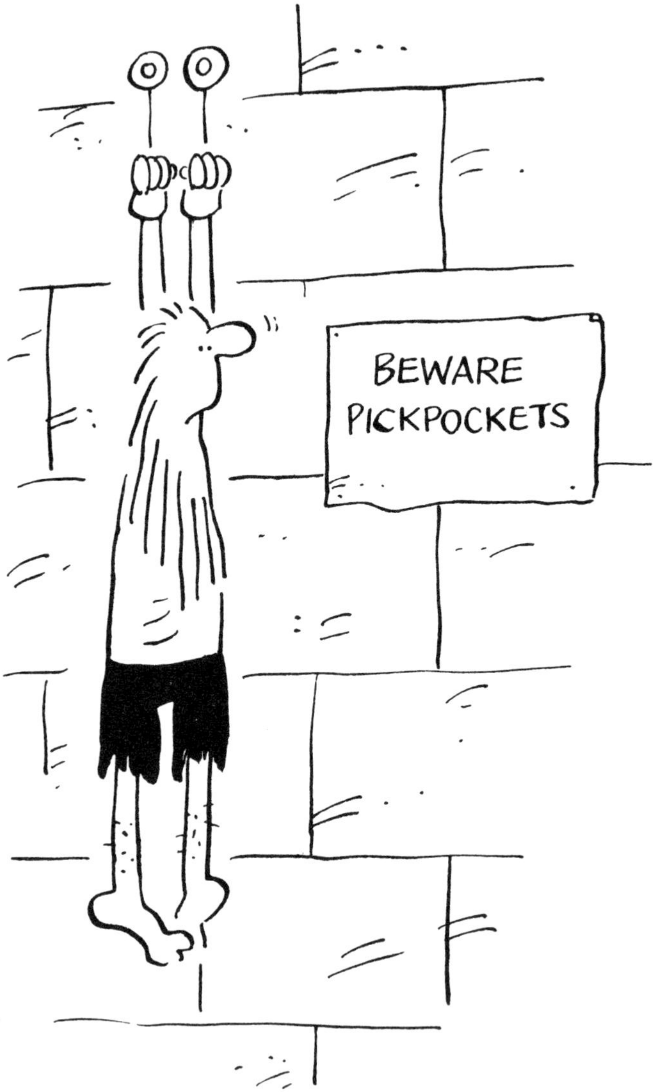
BEWARE
PICKPOCKETS

'Why can't we have plaster ducks, like everyone else?'

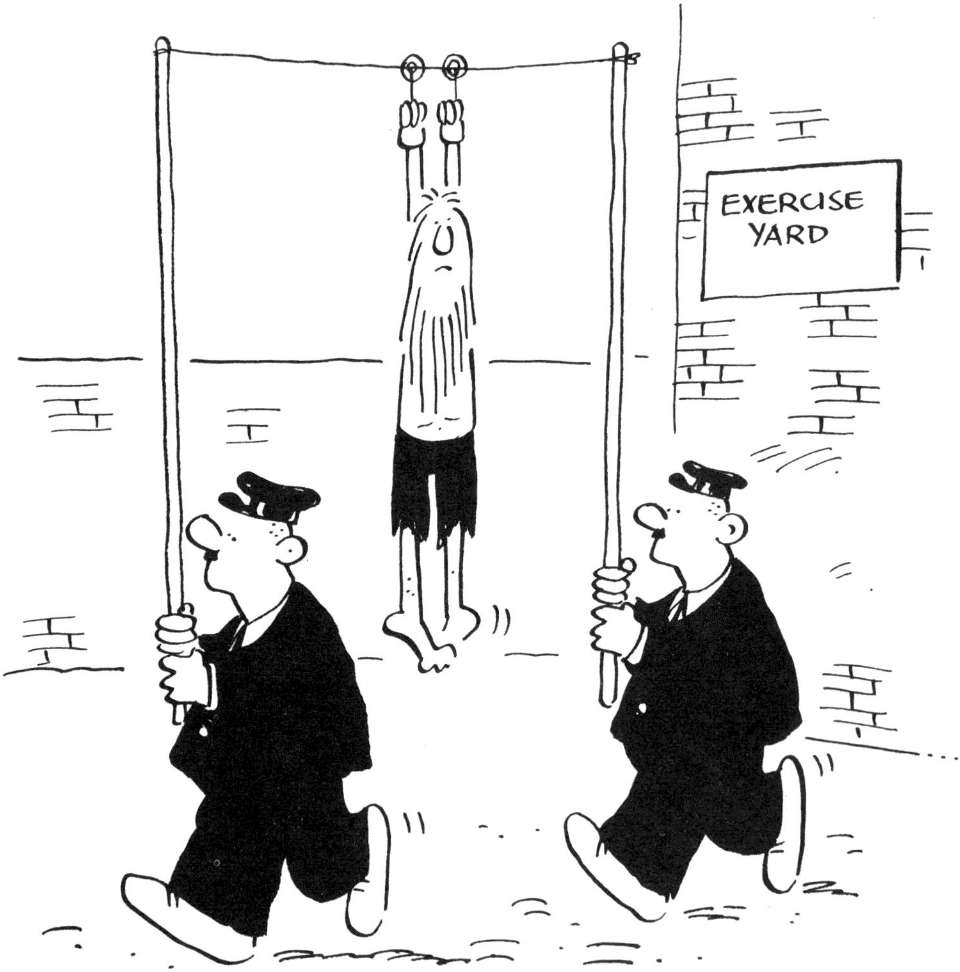
EXERCISE
YARD

'Do we want any double-glazing?'

'...And another thing – you never take me out any more!'

'You put your left leg in, your left leg out – in, out, in, out, shake it
all about...'

'Take no notice – of *course* there's a Father Christmas.'

'There must be an easier way of stock-taking...'

'You've been selected as a contestant on *What's My Line...*'

'Just think — we've missed twenty-seven Eurovision Song
Contests, and at least 150 *Wogan* shows...'

'You've not even *touched* your tapioca!'

'Do we want to buy two tickets for the policeman's ball?'

'...And this is our collection of old masters.'

'Phew! What a nightmare! — I dreamed I was hanging on a wall,
and —'

'Perhaps we should have given him a Christmas tip...'

'The tooth fairy didn't make it again, then?'

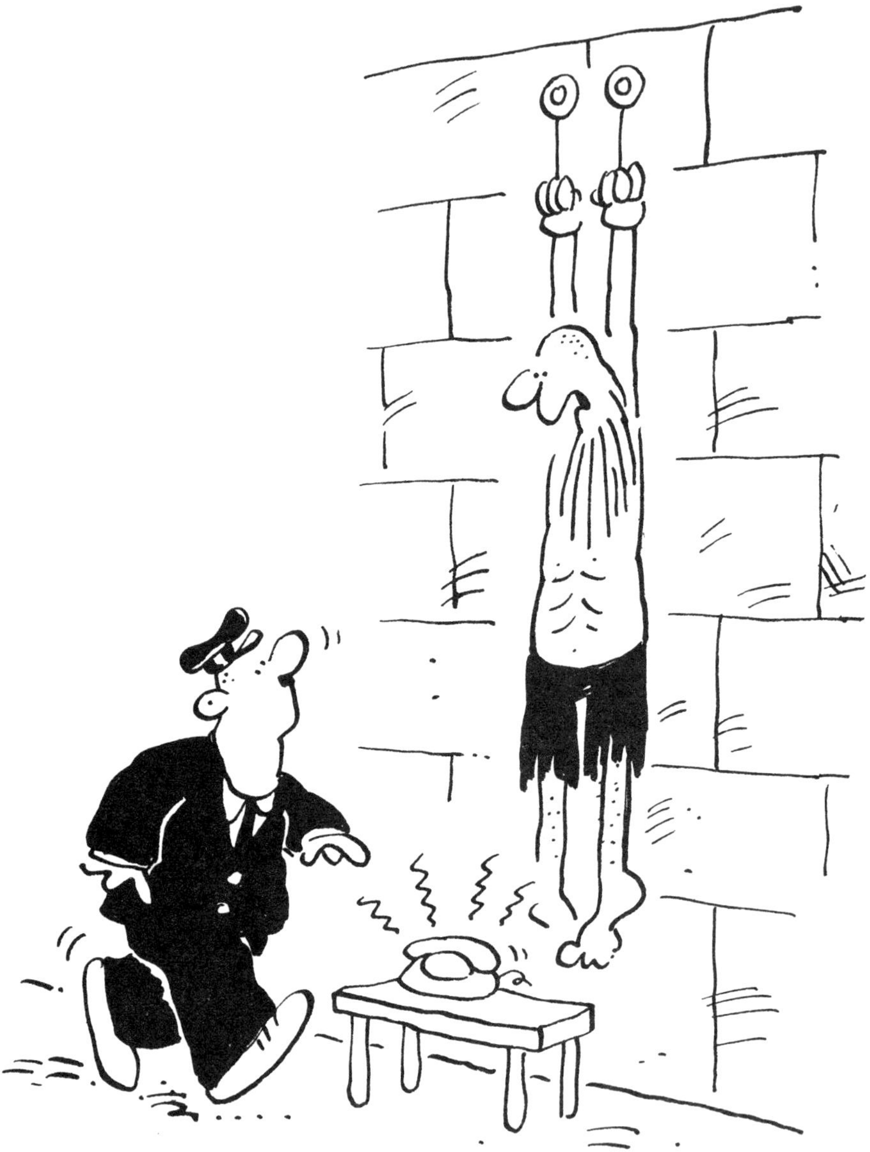

'If that's for me, I'm not in...'

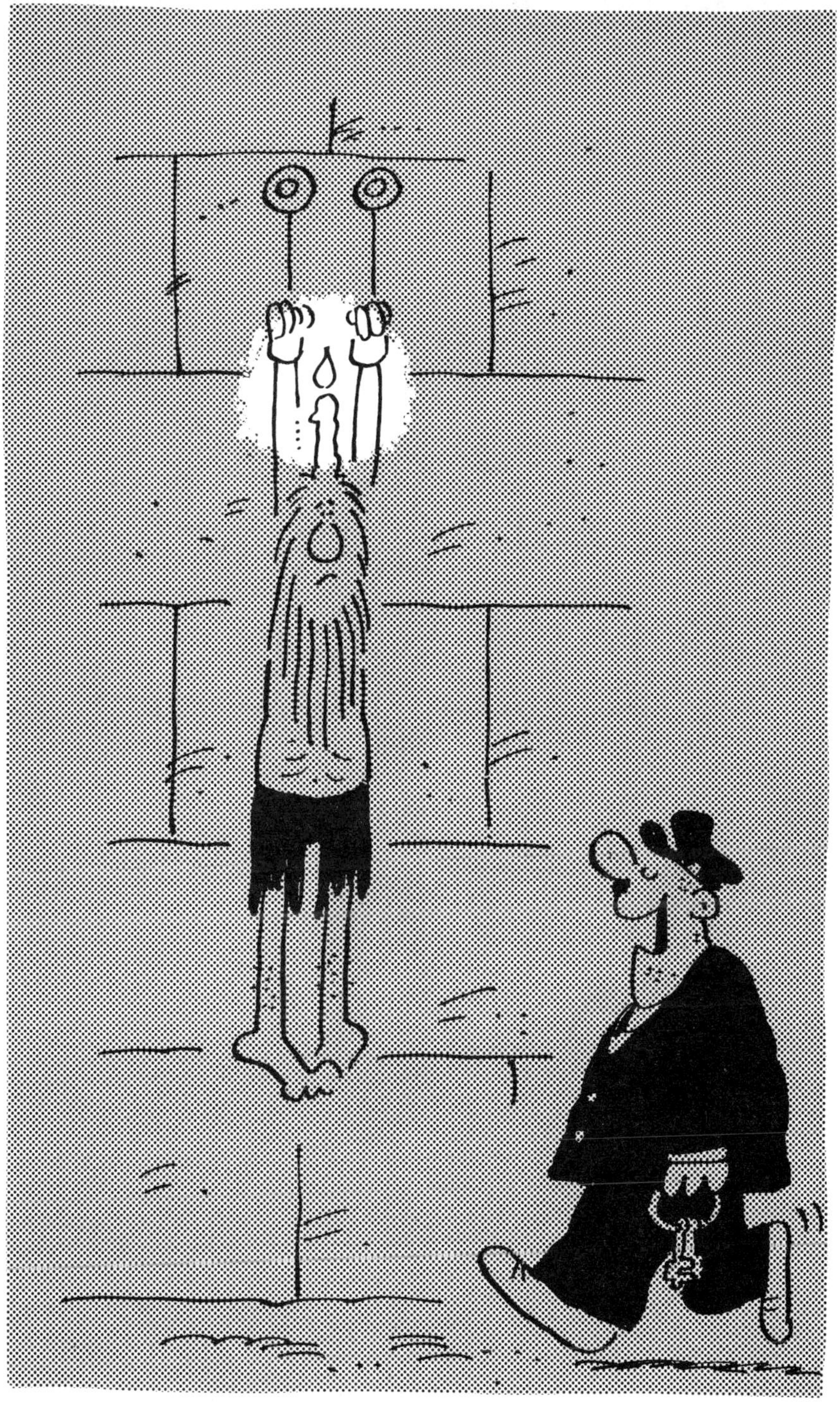

'Lights out!'

'The sparkle seems to have disappeared from our marriage...'

'I thought so – you've got a grey hair...'

'Can you lend me a fiver 'til Thursday?'

'I think they've got the decorators in...'

'*Now* will you go to sleep?'

'What's the social life like round here, fellers?...'

'She's convinced there's another woman.'

'Boy, did you have a restless night!'

'I see they've found you a more cheerful cell...'

'Not *The Prisoner of Zenda* again!'

'There must be an easier way to stop smoking...'

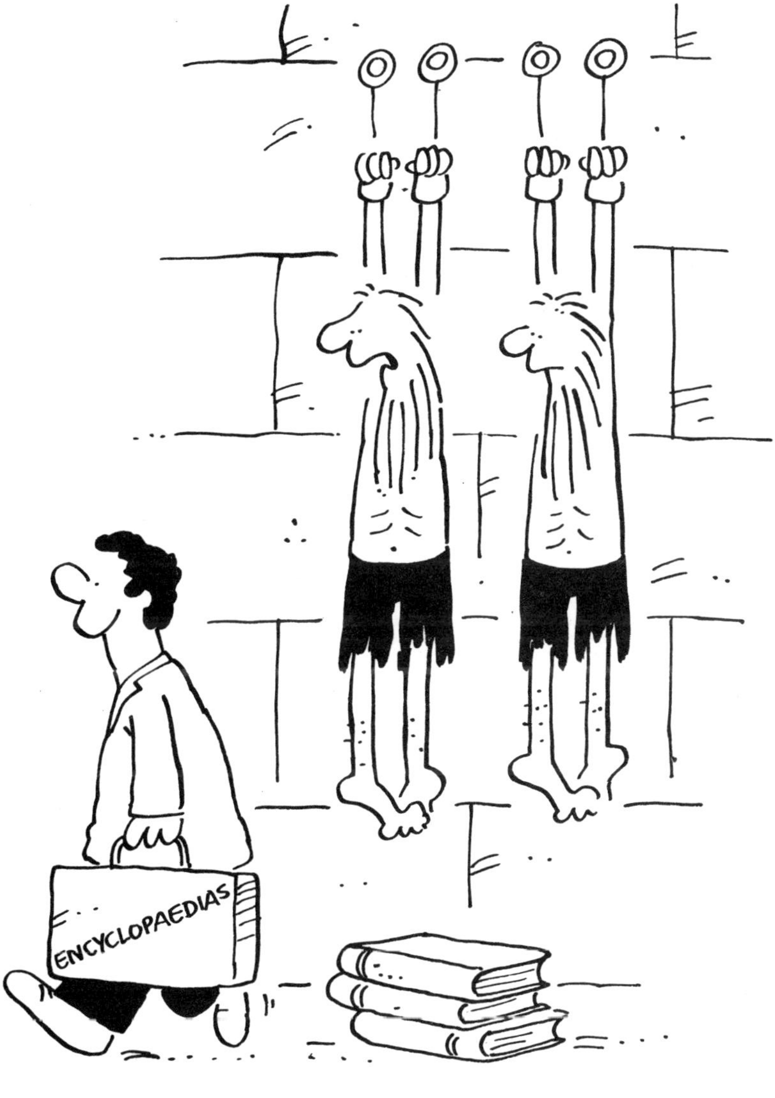
ENCYCLOPAEDIAS

'What a salesman!...'

'Duck!'

'...And they don't need cleaning as often as the brown velvet
ones...'

'Look on the bright side — at least you'll never be made redundant...'

'I think it's time for your early morning alarm call...'

'You'll have to excuse the mess – I've not had a chance to tidy up yet...'

'Well, come on, then – tell me all your news.

'Would you sign for these?'

'No, I don't think it *will* change my life-style...'

'Stop complaining – last year we didn't even *get* a holiday.'

'Good news – the central-heating boiler's been repaired...'

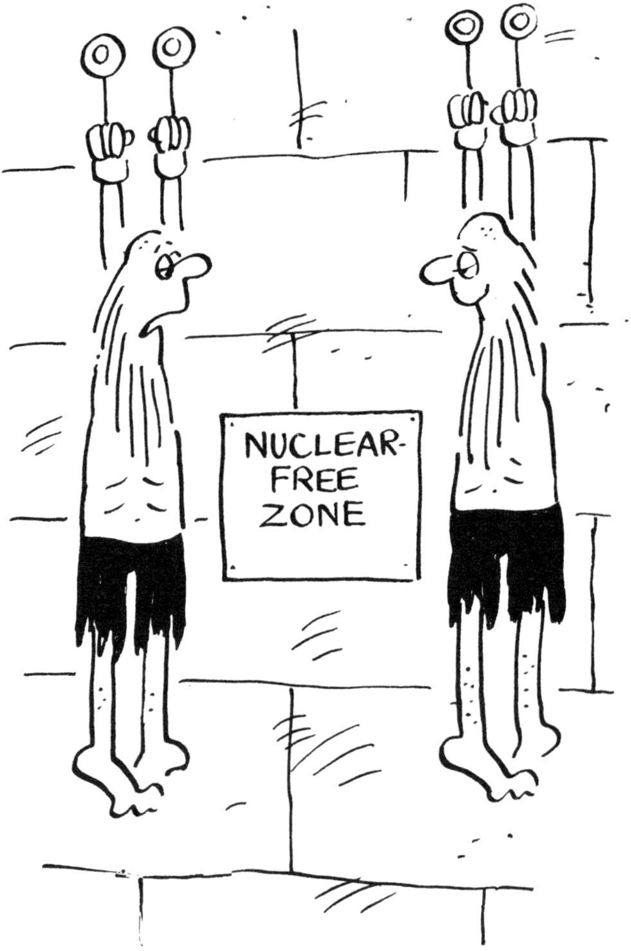
NUCLEAR-
FREE
ZONE

'Comforting, isn't it?'

'Well, it's not *my* idea of a cushy number in the prison library!'

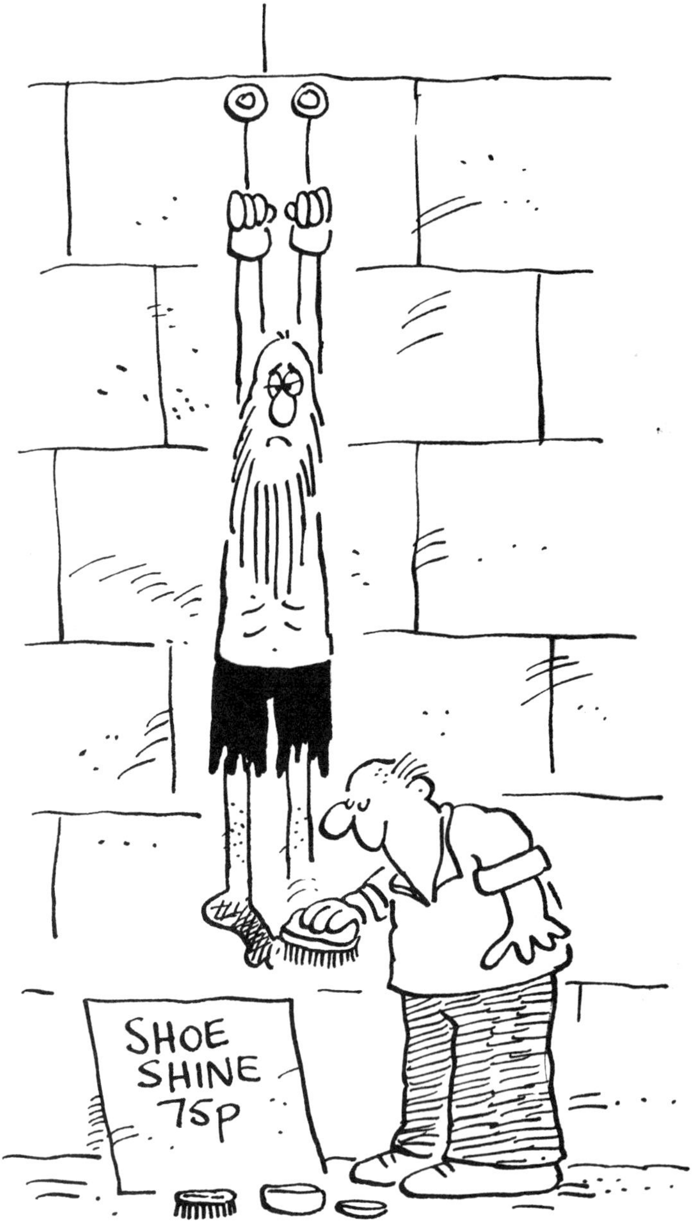
SHOE
SHINE
75p

'Mind you, they say it's *really* getting to you when you start talking to yourself...'

'You must give me the name of your tailor...'

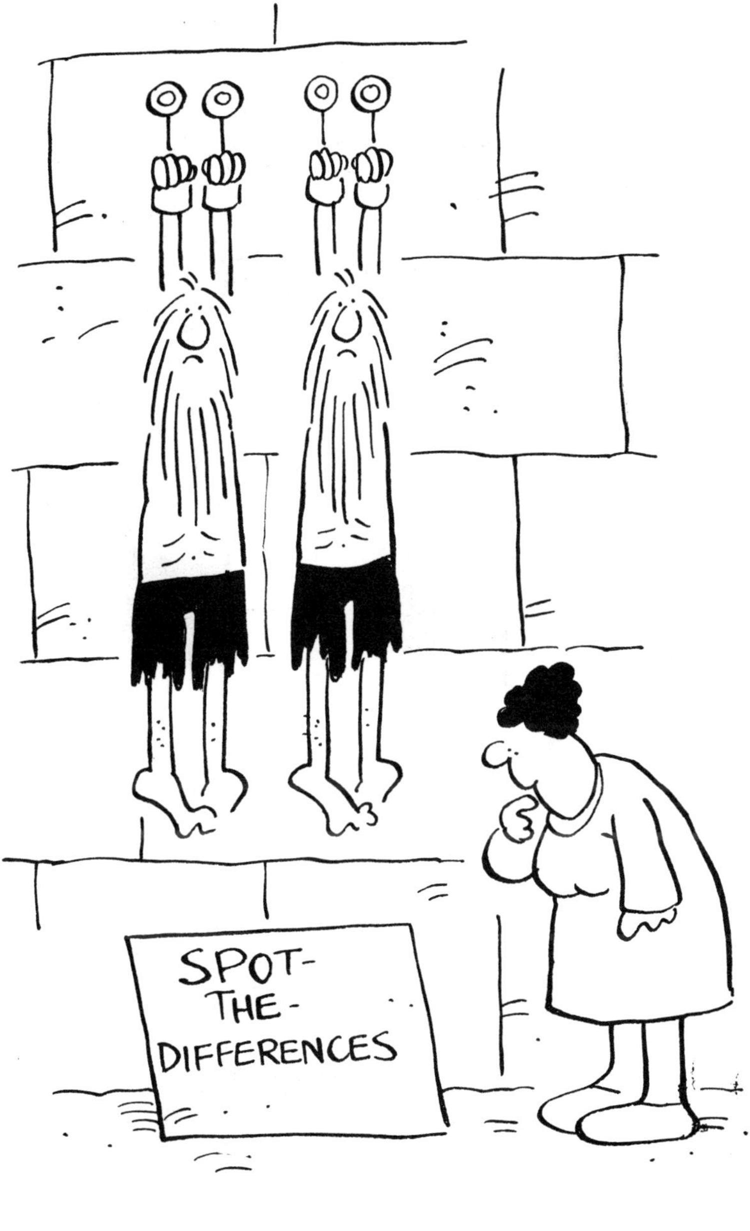
SPOT-
THE-
DIFFERENCES

'I must admit, I've been to livelier discos...'

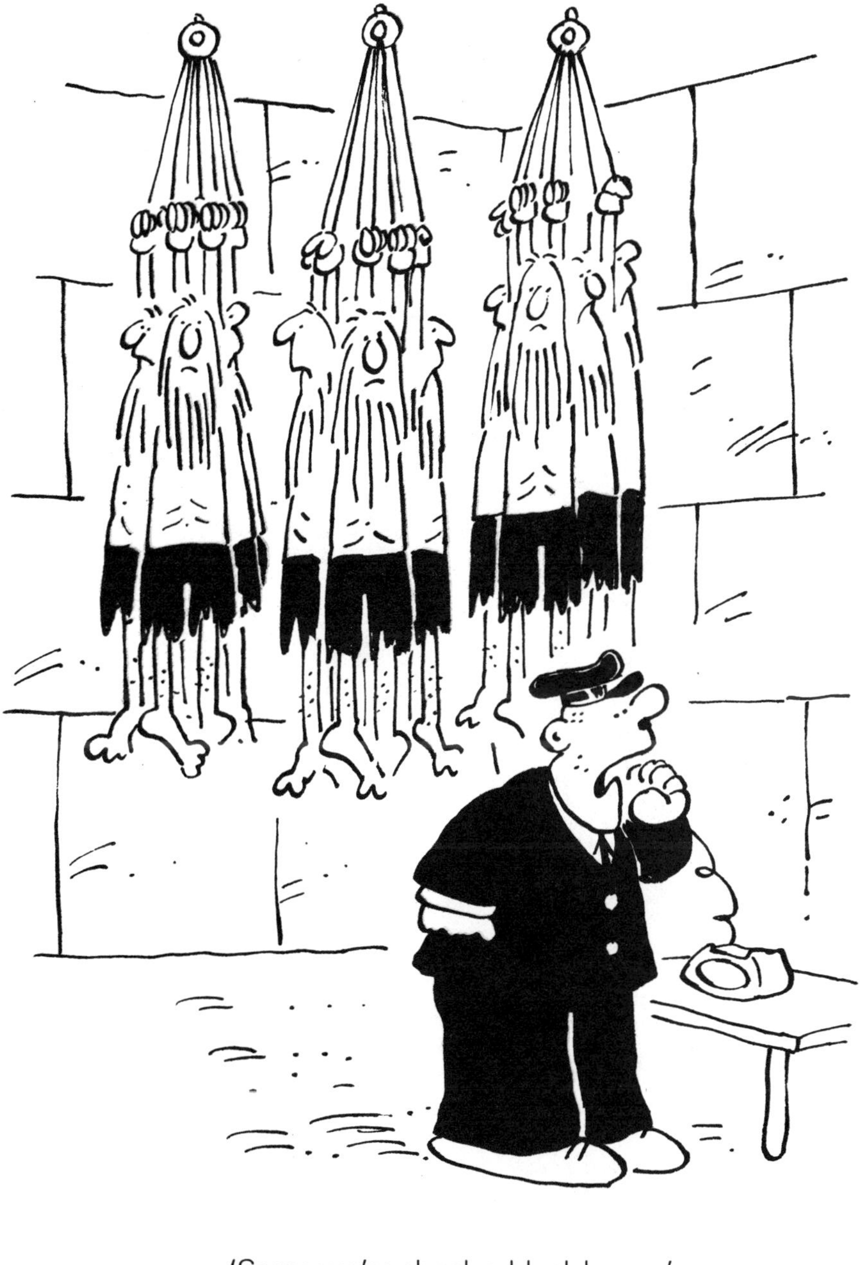

'Sorry, we're chock-a-block here...'

'You know the rules – no pets!'

'They used to be a motor-cycle display team.'

'But I *always* dress for dinner...'

'Not much of a conversationalist, are you?'

'Oh boy! Free at last!'